# Tibet and Shangri-La: The Search for a Hidden Paradise

## By Jesse Harasta and Charles River Editors

A monastery in the Tibetan province of Yunnan. The county is often referred to as Shangri-La County

**Jesse Harasta** graduated in 2009 from Syracuse University with a masters in Linguistic and Cultural Anthropology. Jesse is currently a doctoral student finishing his thesis, and he has had articles published in academic magazines and journals in both the United States and Great Britain.

# Introduction

**Lhasa, the Tibetans' most important city**

"For the valley was nothing less than an enclosed paradise of amazing fertility, in which the vertical difference of a few thousand feet spanned the whole gulf between temperate and tropical" – James Hilton, *Lost Horizon* (1933)

In 1933, British author James Hilton introduced the world to a new destination for journeys of the imagination: the hidden valley of Shangri-La. In doing so, Hilton built upon pre-existing fantasies, stereotypes and archetypes, many of which were centuries old, but Hilton also created something new in the form of a vision which captured the imagination of his contemporaries and has remained ever since. In Hilton's novel, *Lost Horizon*, Shangri-La is a valley high in the north of the Himalayas where a monastery (more accurately, a "lamasery," as the inhabitants were lamas not monks) dedicated to peace and study exists. The precipitously steep valley is also home to a rich variety of flora, and its inhabitants are renowned for their longevity.

The Western myth of Shangri-La is part and parcel of a long-term fascination with Tibet, which even today is still seen as a land of mystery, ancient wisdom and spiritual purity on the roof of the world, all of which stands in contrast to the Western world. Even when *Lost Horizon* was published in 1933, Shangri-La was inseparable from the anxieties of its Western audiences, particularly given the damage done by World War I and the looming World War II.

That said, this does not mean that there are not authentic Tibetan roots for the legend. There is no historical legend of Hilton's "Shangri-La", since the ending "la" means "valley" and "shangri" is a word of Hilton's own invention, but there is a relevant piece of Tibetan mythology: the story of Shambhala. This legendary kingdom exists outside (to the north) of Tibet and represents the "pure land" of Buddhist and harmonious living. The story of Shambhala may have influenced Hilton's original work, but it has undoubtedly had an influence on later writing and imaginations of the place.

*Tibet and Shangri-La: The Search for a Hidden Paradise* explores the history of Tibet and legend of Shangri-La from the mists of Tibetan pre-history and traces the history of the idea as it became fused with Buddhism and was tied to the idea of a Pure Land. This book also looks at the West's encounter with Tibet in the early 20th century, including both expeditions and literature that described and popularized Shangri-La in Romantic poems, pulp novels and popular esoteric mysticism. Finally, the book traces the way in which Tibetan culture has moved west and influenced the globe. Along with footnotes, a bibliography and pictures, you will learn about Shangri-La like you never have before, in no time at all.

## A Discussion of Names

In this book, the terms "Shangri-La" and "Shambhala" will not be used interchangeably. The use of Shambhala will be in reference to the stories, myths and images that emerged out of a Tibetan and Tibetan-Buddhist context, while Shangri-La will refer to those versions of the story that emerged out of the West, including the literature that predates the 1933 publication of *Lost Horizon*, the novel that gave the idea and place its famous name. The terms became mixed after the Chinese invasion of Tibet in 1951 and with further Western access to the region, but the differentiation of terms still serves a useful purpose.

## Chapter 1: The Roof of the World

In order to understand how the myth of Shambhala emerged and how it was adopted and interpreted by Westerners to become the Shangri-La legend known today, it is necessary to first understand something about Tibet, the story's homeland. Tibet is sometimes called the "Roof of the World" due to its location along the northern side of the Himalaya mountains in the Tibetan Plateau, one of the world's highest regions. Naturally, this has also made it a tremendously isolated region, with the Himalayas to the south, the Karakoram mountains to the west, the great Taklamakan desert and the Kunlun Mountains to the north and a rough land of gorges and broken rocky terrain to the east. It is the world's highest and largest plateau and has a major meteorological impact on the rest of Asia. The rugged geography facilitated the creation of the Shambhala and Shangri-La myths, because the region was so complex and travel was so difficult that it was (and is) easy to imagine hidden valleys, secret monasteries and hidden traditions.

At the same time, Tibet lies at the juncture of several ancient empires, with India to the south, China to the east, Persia to the west and the Mongols and eventually the Russians to the north. Ultimately, the region, literature and mythology were all influenced from those four directions and molded the way in which the myth was imagined, retold and translated. Much of Tibet's 20th century history involves an ultimately unsuccessful attempt to balance the power of the Russians, Chinese and British in India, all of whom were either fascinated by the Shambhala stories or used to their advantage, but even in earlier times, there were subtle influences coming from the four directions, including Bon (potentially from Persia) and Buddhism from India. These influences came together with the foreign and mysterious nature of the terrain to fuel both Tibetan and Western imaginations, and it's indeed fair to say that legend drew upon reality in some respects. For example, Buddhism itself hid away in isolated monasteries during the collapse of the Tibetan Empire, as did the Bon tradition during the height of Buddhist authority in Lhasa.

The Tibetans themselves are a highly distinctive people whose differences from their neighbors sparked the imaginations of 20th century visitors from places like Germany who imagined ancient kinship to the fictitious Aryan race. The "Tibetan language" is actually a family of roughly 81 interrelated languages spoken not only in Tibet but also Nepal, Bhutan, India, other areas of China, and even Pakistan. "Central Tibetan," the largest branch and the one spoken by the Dalai Lama and the Buddhist religious institutions, had almost 1.2 million speakers in 1990[1]. While the Tibetan languages are distantly related to lowland Chinese dialects, speakers of Mandarin cannot understand Tibetans and vice-versa, and it was not traditionally considered one of the forms of Chinese. The Tibetans did not traditionally use Chinese characters for writing, instead developing an alphabet based off of the Devanagari script of India used for Sanskrit[2].

**A map of the region**

While today the Tibetans are known for their practice of the ostensibly pacifist religion of Buddhism, this was not always the case. The early Tibetans practiced other faiths, including the worship of mountain gods, and this ancient religion was blended first with the faith known today as Bon (further discussed below) coming from the west. In the 700s, the Tibetans ruled a widespread Tibetan Empire led by noble Bon-worshiping families, but this was followed by a period of fragmentation and civil war that allowed Buddhism to begin to take root amongst the people. Ultimately, it was not until the region was brought into the Mongol Empire in the 1200s that Buddhism began to spread widely and the Dalai Lama lineage was established. By the 1600s, the Buddhist monks had established enough power within the wreckage of the Mongol Empire to make themselves the political, as well as spiritual, leaders of Tibet.

The incorporation of Tibet into the Mongol Empire initiated the most important political dynamic in modern Tibetan history: the relationship between China and Tibet. After the fall of the Mongols, the

1    "Central Tibetan: A Language of China" at the *Ethnologue: Languages of the World* website. Accessed online at: http://www.ethnologue.com/language/bod
2    "Tibetan" at the *Omniglot: The Online Encyclopedia of Writing Systems and Languages* website. Accessed online at: http://www.omniglot.com/writing/tibetan.htm

region has moved pendulum-style back and forth between being a semi-autonomous part of the Chinese Empire and being an independent state. The Chinese emperors recognized Tibet as distinctive amongst all of the parts of their dominions and often consulted the Dalai Lamas in spiritual matters, giving the Tibetans considerable leeway to rule their dominions. Moreover, when Chinese dynasties fell or China was divided by civil war, it was unable to exercise power over Tibet and other peripheral areas, especially Mongolia, meaning the area enjoyed independence in practice if not in name. However, when the Chinese consolidated power under a single dynasty or regime, they have tended to reign in Tibet and other outlying areas.

At the same time that Tibet oscillated between Chinese control and independence, the Tibetan Buddhist faith, which had developed much of its distinctiveness in relation to Bon, began to spread widely across central Asia and led many of the peoples of the continent to look to the Tibetan capital of Lhasa for guidance. Perhaps the most important group to acknowledge the Dalai Lama, and the ones most important to the story of Shambhala/Shangri-La, are the Mongolians of today's Mongolia and China. Traditionally ruled by a Dalai Lama-like Buddhist figure, they have embraced the legend of Shambhala as their own, a belief that was used against them in the early 20th century by the imperial powers struggling over control of Asia. Other Tibetan Buddhist groups include the monarchies of Bhutan and Sikkim (today annexed by India), many of the ethnicities of Nepal and the people of Ladakh (a region divided between India and Pakistan). In today's Russia there are several Tibetan Buddhist ethnicities, including the Buryats, Tuvans and Kalmykians.

At one time, Buddhist kingdoms were much more widespread in Central Asia, including the builders of the famous Bamiyan Buddha statues destroyed by the Afghan Taliban regime in 2001,[3] but in most areas, Buddhism has retreated before the expansion of Islam, especially amongst Turkish-speaking peoples, though in India it has been replaced by Hinduism. This retreat has also been important to the development of the Shambhala myth, since it has a distinctly martial character and the prophesied invaders have often been interpreted as being the followers of Mohammed.

---

3   "Bamiyan Valley" accessed online at: http://www.sacredland.org/bamiyan-valley/

**Buddhist flags flying in the Himalayas**

## Chapter 2: The Roots of Shambhala

"Although those with special affiliation may actually be able to go there through their karmic connection, nevertheless it is not a physical place that we can actually find. We can only say that it is a pure land, a pure land in the human realm. And unless one has the merit and the actual karmic association, one cannot actually arrive there." - The 14th Dalai Lama on Shambhala

The exact origins of Shambhala have not survived in writing due to the lack of writing in pre-Buddhist Tibet, due in part to the incredible difficulty that the Himalayas - not to mention the deserts that surround them to the north - present for traveling. Of course, the inability of other cultures with writing to reach Tibet also made it possible for them to imagine hidden valleys and lost cultures, both of which have been staples of stories in the region. Some of these tales can be traced to the Tibetan faith tradition that is today called "Bon."

According to the 14th Dalai Lama[4], Bon is the "ancient, indigenous religious and cultural tradition of our ancestors, which is the source and embodiment of many aspects of the Tibetan way of life."[5] This tradition is said to have originated in the west of modern-day Tibet in a kingdom called Olmo Lungring. Bon is undoubtedly the coalescence of centuries of development within the Tibetan culture, but its beliefs and practices were formalized by Tonpa Shenrab, a figure who holds a status very similar to that of the Buddha in Buddhism.[6]

---

4  The 14th Dalai Lama is the current leader of Tibetan Buddhism was born in 1935 and has reigned since 1950.
5  "Letter from the H.H. The Dalai Lama", accessed online at the Bon Foundation Homepage:
   http://www.bonfoundation.org/letter.html

**A depiction of Tonpa Shenrab**

However, Bon was eventually displaced as the primary religious system of the Tibetan people by the arrival of Buddhism, a philosophy first developed in modern-day India, and over time, the Buddhists came to dominate Tibet spiritual, politically and socially. Despite centuries of (at times overt) repression by Buddhists, as well as by the Chinese Communist regime since 1950, Bon continues to be practiced in both Tibet and amongst the Tibetan Diaspora. Importantly for the survival of Bon into the era of Diaspora, where it is separated from its traditional base in folk traditions and ancient monasteries, there was a recognition of the legitimacy and importance of this element of Tibetan tradition by the Dalai Lama himself during a 1978 visit to a newly-built Bon monastery in northern India. Today, there has been a growing rapprochement between Buddhism and Bon; for instance, the monks of each of the four traditional schools of Tibetan Buddhism elects two representatives to the Parliament of the Central Tibetan Administration, and today the Bonpo also elect the holders of two seats.

Moreover, despite a long term hostility, Tibetan Buddhism actually gained much of its distinctiveness by borrowing concepts and practices from Bon, and Bon in turn borrowed heavily from Buddhism.

6   "About Bon and Menri" accessed online at the Bon Foundation: http://www.bonfoundation.org/aboutbon.html

One of the most important of these concepts was the legend of Shambhala itself. For the Bonpo (practitioners of Bon), the land of their faith's origin - Olmo Lungring - is the source of the tale of Shambhala: a legendary and ancient kingdom to the north and/or west of Tibet ruled over by wise and just kings.[7] Sometimes it is known as "Tagzig Olmo Lungring," because it was said to exist within a larger region of Tagzig.

Olmo Lungring is said to be both a physical place on the Earth (debatably a Himalayan valley, Central Asia or Iran) and simultaneously an "imperishable" kingdom that is not of this world. The Earthly version is a copy or a shadow of the true version that merely represents the best approximation that humans can create of the divine realm. This place, in both of its aspects, serves as the conduit between heaven and earth; here the gods descend and rule amongst humans as kings, and it is to this land that spiritual seekers journey to gain wisdom to bring back to the rest of humanity. It is rumored that some of these sages live on eternally in Olmo Lungring, preserving ancient wisdom, and that someday far in the future, when the world has descended into purity and wisdom, a great sage or leader will emerge from Olmo Lungring to restore the world[8]. Olmo Lungring is also seen as the spiritual heart at the center of each human being, a place accessed through the meditative arts and depicted in elaborate sand art and paintings[9]. All of these elements found their way in some form into the eventual myth of Shambhala.

Tibet and the Himalayas, despite their isolation, have never been completely cut off culturally and religiously from the rest of Asia, so it's perhaps not surprising that the myth of Olmo Lungring and the Bon tradition in general appears to contain echoes of a cultural exchange with the Persian Empire's culture to the west. The eventual importation of Buddhism was a cultural influence from India to the south, but there was also cultural influence coming from the east in the form of China. Chinese Folk Religion, which long dominated Imperial China but was largely destroyed in the Chinese Civil War and Communist Cultural Revolution, also developed a tradition about an imperishable realm known as Penglai Mountain or Penglai Island. It was the home of the legendary Eight Immortals, human beings who reached a level of Daoist perfection and ceased aging, thereby becoming more akin to gods than humans. The mountain had eight peaks, each with a palace of one of the immortals, and was surrounded by a sea of rippling air that was akin to water. The only way to reach it was by flight. At the same time, it was also said to be an actual, physical island existing within the Sea of Bohai off the coast of today's northeast China[10].

There are a number of similarities between the Bon's Olmo Lungring and the Chinese's Penglai Island. The first is that both are thought to be simultaneously divine locales and also physical places that exist on Earth in geographically distant and isolated area. Furthermore, each is thought to be ruled by individuals that cross over between the divine and the human, and these rulers then serve as conduits for sacred power and wisdom to enter the human world at large. A major difference is that Olmo Lungring was also seen as being a spiritual location within the individual worshiper that could be

---

7   http://www.surajamrita.com/bon/Shambala.html
8   "Olmo Lung-Ring: The Imperishable Sacred Land" accessed online at: http://www.surajamrita.com/bon/Shambala.html
9   For examples of Olmo Lungring in Tibetan art, visit: http://www.himalayanart.org/search/set.cfm?setID=1041
10  "Penglai Shan." (1996). In *Bloomsbury Dictionary of Myth*. Accessed online at:
    http://www.credoreference.com.libezproxy2.syr.edu/entry/bloommyth/penglai_shan

accessed through meditation and ritual.

The myth of Shambhala as it has been passed down came from the esoteric Tibetan Buddhist texts called the "Kalachakra". The texts claim the land of Shambhala, which ranges in size from a village to a kingdom, exists to the north and/or west of Tibet. This is a place of Buddhist spiritual perfection, made so because the first king of Shambhala brought the Buddha's Kalachakra teachings with him when he arrived. His descendants rule the kingdom for the six subsequent generations, and the seventh king shall unite all of the castes and take the title of "Kalki," the name of an avatar of the god Vishnu. Then more centuries and generations pass, until in the 25th generation. In this time, invaders will arrive from outside the Buddhist world and will threaten everything with destruction. At that time, the current Kalki (the title passes from father to son) will emerge from his hiding place in Shambhala to lead the forces of that nation and drive back the invaders, thereby establishing a new era of peace and Buddhist glory for all people.

Although today "Buddhism" and "Hinduism" are considered two separate religions, the idea that they are mutually exclusive and distinct is a relatively recent development, in large part due to the desire of the British colonial masters to classify, tabulate and organize all of the "religions" of India in their census and government policies. Before this time, there was considerable overlap between the two, and today Buddhism can be thought of as an outgrowth of the Hindu milieu[11]. Thus, the appearance of the figure of Kalki in an ostensibly "Buddhist" tale is not surprising. Kalki was originally a sun-god who came to be viewed as an avatar of the great god Vishnu (who is the preserver of the world). He was the tenth avatar of Vishnu, and it was written that his appearance on the world would presage an apocalyptic battle, the world's destruction, and the birth of a new golden age[12].

---

11  *Religion, Science and Empire: Classifying Hinduism and Islam in British India* (2012) by Peter Gottschalk, Oxford University Press.
12  "Kalki" in the *Mythology Dictionary*, accessed online at: http://www.mythologydictionary.com/kalki-mythology.html

This myth fuses several elements from the various neighboring cultures, including the Tibetan indigenous Bon tradition of Olmo Lungring, earlier Hindu scriptures (there are earlier, pre-Buddhist references to Kalki as an avatar ruling a land called Shambhala), and Buddhist teachings. This mixture is a reflection of Tibetan Buddhism in general, which always blends these various strands into a single, harmonious whole. This prophecy has important elements that have continued to emerge in the times since, including the position of Shambhala to the north and west, the messianic military leader, the threat of invasion and the promised golden age.

For many who view Buddhism and, especially Tibetan Buddhism, as a religion of peace and harmony, the myth of Shambhala and its prophecies of apocalyptic war and destruction seems jarring. While Islam has often been criticized for its concept of *jihad*, or holy struggle, this is a concept that is not alien to Buddhism as well. The first Buddha was originally a warrior, and he did not shy away from occasional military metaphors; in jihad as well, the military metaphor is often used to discuss an internal spiritual struggle. Fittingly, during the era when Islamic invaders from the west threatened the Buddhist kingdoms of modern-day Afghanistan, Pakistan and northern India, the Shambhala myth and predictions about invasion and war became a popular element of Buddhist thought.[13]

## Chapter 3: The Valley as the Pure Land

According to the current Dalai Lama, Shambhala is not primarily a real-world physical place but instead a spiritual state achieved through meditation and "karmic connection." He does not deny that there may have been a place on Earth that corresponded to it in legend, but that those who seek it should look inside themselves rather than in the northern Himalayan valleys.

Shambhala in this sense is an example of a tradition called "Pure Land Buddhism", "a flexible network of texts, terms, ideas, and images most commonly related to conceptions of a future realm of existence alternate to our present world." In this realm, the worshiper encounters a Buddha - traditionally Ö-pa-me in Tibet (or, "Amitābha" in Sanskrit, "Amida" in Japanese, and "Omito-fo" in Chinese), the Buddha of Infinite Light, who aids the worshiper in his or her path to enlightenment. The Pure Land itself, as well as the central Buddha figure within it, serve as tools for enlightenment, a tradition of Buddhism that is very different from the individual-worshiper focus in traditions like Zen that are often more familiar to Western audiences[14].

One of the important texts in Tibetan Buddhism is the Kalachakra Tantra, said to be an esoteric teaching of the Buddha himself. Kalachakra is a tradition of meditation and mystical study where students are initiated into advanced levels of study, and it has a direct link to Shambhala. The story maintains that the Buddha taught the Kalachakra at a request from Sucandra, the king of Shambhala, and that it was transmitted from there up to the Himalayas and preserved amongst the people of that kingdom. The story continues that it was brought back to India in the 10th century and then to Tibet

---

13 "Holy Wars in Buddhism and Islam: The Myth of Shambhala" by Alexander Berzin (2003). Accessed online at the Berzin Archives:
   http://www.berzinarchives.com/web/en/archives/study/islam/kalachakra_islam/holy_wars_buddhism_islam_myth_shamb/holy_war_buddhism_islam_shambhala_long.html
14 "Pure Land Buddhism" (2010) in *Buddhism* by Galen Amstutz. Oxford University Press.

from there, where the original Sanskrit was translated to Tibetan[15].

The Tantra text teaches how the student moves from the outer world, to the inner and finally to the spiritual, enlightened realm.  This enlightened realm has also been associated with the land of Shambhala.[16]  One of the most important artistic traditions in Tibet has been the creation of mandalas: paintings or sand art images that depict symbolic representations of cities, palaces, or kingdoms which the devotee uses as a meditative tool (often by meditating while creating the image).  The devotee imagines entering and exploring the rooms of the image, which are linked to philosophical concepts in the Kalachakra tantra.  Many of these images are purported to depict Shambhala, which serves as a meditative tool for the believer, much as it does in the concept of the Buddhist Pure Land.[17]  These colorful, symmetrical works of art are often masterpieces of Tibetan culture.

15 "Introduction to Kalacakra", accessed online at: http://www.kalacakra.org/aboutk.htm
16 "Shambhala: Myths and Reality" from the Berzin Archives, accessed online:
   http://www.berzinarchives.com/web/en/archives/advanced/kalachakra/shambhala/shambhala_myths_reality/transcript.html
17 "Shambhala - The Magic Kingdom" accessed online at: http://kalachakranet.org/kalachakra_tantra_shambhala.html

**A 17th century Tibetan mandela**

# Chapter 4: The Roots of Western Interest

"In Xanadu did Kubla Khan

A stately pleasure-dome decree:

Where Alph, the sacred river, ran

Through caverns measureless to man

Down to a sunless sea" - From *Kubla Khan* by Samuel Taylor Coleridge (1816)

"He ... shall descend on Earth as an outstanding Brahman from Shambhala ... endowed with the eight superhuman faculties. Through his irresistible power he will ... destroy all whose hearts have been relinquished to evil. He will re-establish righteousness on earth." – H.P. Blavatsky, *The Secret Doctrine*, vol. 1, (1888)

For much of history, the Western world has been ignorant of the Shambhala myth, given that its believers were located thousands of miles away in the Tibetan Buddhist lands of Tibet, Mongolia, Buryatia, Tuva and Kalmykia. In fact, even other Buddhist lands, including China, Sri Lanka and Japan, were ignorant of the myth. However, beginning in the early 19th century Westerners began to take an interest in the "Orient," and in Buddhism and Buddhist philosophy. During this period, Tibet became a fascination for many Westerners, and with that, they began to become interested in the myth of Shambhala. This interest began in the area of literature and then religion, particularly amongst the believers of the Theosophical Society, and over time, information became more concrete, especially after the British Expedition to Tibet in 1903-1904.

The idea of a beautiful, Oriental paradise existing on Earth was not new in 1933 but dates back to Orientalist writers of the Romantic movement. The Orientalists used the Orient, which included everything from Morocco to Japan, as the stage for their own fantasies, inverting the social order of Europe to, at worst, simply titillate their audiences with racial stereotypes and, at best, to explore the possibility of the human imagination and the best of human potential. Of the many archetypes these writers developed, one of them was the exotic, morally pure and beautiful Oriental paradise. Perhaps the most famous example of this phenomenon was Samuel Taylor Coleridge's 1816 poem *Kubla Khan, or A Vision in a Dream. A Fragment.* The poem is famous not only for its content but also for the story behind it. When it was published, the poem included a background story: Coleridge was sleeping (presumably off of a laudanum high) and had an incredible dream. Upon waking, he feverishly sat down to write everything he saw in his dream; however, he was disturbed by "a person from Porlock" (a nearby village) who so distracted him from his writing that he lost the memory and left the poem unfinished.

The poem itself describes a pleasure palace called "Xanadu" built by the great Mongol/Chinese emperor Kubla Khan, a ruler made famous in the West by the breathless writings of Marco Polo. Xanadu is described as an Edenic heaven-on-earth separated from the rest of the world by high walls[18].

Another influence was the widely popular "Lost World" genre. Since the publication of *King Solomon's Mines* in 1885, the Western world (especially in English) had enjoyed a fascination with the idea of lost cities. Heinrich Schliemann's excavations at Troy from the 1860s, Hiram Bingham's "discovery" of Machu Picchu in 1911, Arthur Conan Doyle's publication of *The Lost World* (1912) and Edgar Rice Burrough's *The Land that Time Forgot* (1918) all boosted the public's interest in ancient civilizations, a tendency which Hilton's 1933 *Lost Horizon* (where the term "Shangri-La" was introduced) built upon. Hilton's work was within this genre both in its content and its style, though it innovated in making Shangri-La's wealth be of a spiritual and mystical variety rather than the gemstones of King Solomon's Mine or the jewels found by Schliemann. The wistful nature of the book and the lead characters' search for meaning and enlightenment in Eastern philosophy was very much en vogue in the era after World War I, when many were turning to Buddhism for.

The Romantic and pulp literature certainly laid the groundwork culturally for an interest in Oriental lost civilizations, but much of the credit for the eventual popularity of Shangri-La must be given to Helena Blavatsky (1831-1891) and the Theosophical Society she created. Like many of those who brought the story of Shambhala to the Western world, Helena was born within the Russian Empire and traveled widely throughout her life. In 1875, while in New York City, she became one of the founders of the Theosophical Society, and she went on to publish a major work called *Isis Unveiled* in 1877 and then her most important piece, *The Secret Doctrine*, in 1888.

---

18 Full text of the poem can be found here:
http://www.gutenberg.org/catalog/world/readfile?fk_files=48043&pageno=58

**Blavatsky**

Blavatsky described herself as a missionary for a group of hidden masters she called the "Mahatmas" or "Adepts" or "Ascended Masters", a secret society of enlightened (and possibly immortal) Asian masters who preserved the wisdom of the world. Blavatsky's "theosophy" drew heavily upon Buddhist teachings and served to lay the groundwork for the fascination with Buddhism in many sectors of the West in the 20th century, as well as some Buddhist Reform movements in Asia itself.[19]

The Ascended Masters were said to live in hidden fastnesses from which they communicated with the rest of the world, and Blavatasky identified three locations for their homes: Luxor on the Upper Nile, Shigatse in Tibet (famous as the home of the Panchen Lama and the second-most important city after Lhasa) and Shambhala. Her followers continued and expanded her work and interest in Tibetan culture, most famously by translating and popularizing the text largely known since then as the "*Tibetan Book of the Dead*," which has since been popular with Westerners like Timothy Leary, Alan Ginsberg and William Burroughs[20].

---

19 "H.P. Blavatsky and the Theosophical Society" (2001), accessed online at
   http://www.theosociety.org/pasadena/gfk-lamp/lamps-14.htm
20 "Ride the Tiger," accessed online at http://www.guardian.co.uk/books/2005/oct/22/highereducation.classics

**A picture of Shigatse in 2009**

The British had been a colonial power in India since the late 17th century, but the golden age of their power in the subcontinent came about in the late 19th and early 20th centuries, after the consolidation of power to the Crown in 1857.[21] For the British, the most powerful empire in the world at that time, India was their "crown jewel", and they were willing to expend massive amounts of treasure and military power to protect it. Most famously, they fought a series of wars in Afghanistan from 1839-1919, but they also competed with the Russians for influence across the Asian continent, a standoff that has come to be known as the "Great Game." The two great powers sought to capitalize on the crumbling of two older empires: China and Persia.

It was perhaps inevitable that Tibet, caught between India, Russia, Persia and China, would be drawn into this competition, and in that sense it's somewhat surprising that this only occurred as late as 1903, no doubt due to the region's isolation. Officially, the British became aware of a rumor that the Dalai Lama was hosting Russian envoys and determined to launch a punitive expedition into the Himalayan country.

The mission was relatively short-lived, as the troops returned in 1904 and never brought Tibet under British control, but it did have other long-term effects. The first was that it "opened" Tibet to Western trade and influence, thus bringing a large number of Westerners into the holy city of Lhasa for the first time. A second effect was that when word of the British invasion reached the

---

21 After the Rebellion of that year, known as the Sepoy Rebellion in Britain and the First Indian War of Independence in India.

ears of the court in Beijing, the Qing Dynasty sent out a second expedition - which arrived in Lhasa in 1910 - to bring the region back to heel. This was after a long period a relative autonomy for Tibet, but the Chinese domination was short-lived as well because the Qing government collapsed during the Chinese Revolution of 1913, allowing Tibet to regain its independence. Nevertheless, it strengthened later claims by the People's Republic of China over the region. Meanwhile, both invasions left a deep distrust of outsiders amongst the Tibetan leadership that would only heighten during the coming era, when foreign expeditions regularly arrived in Lhasa bringing the promises of outside powers.[22]

**A view of Lhasa from the Pabonka Monastery**

The British also took plenty away from the 1903 Expedition, including concrete experiences in Tibet and Lhasa, a firsthand account of Tibetan Buddhism, and, possibly the ever-growing myth of Shambhala. This interest would blossom into a fascination for many Westerners in the coming years, especially in the wake of the 1913 Revolution, when the region once again became available for visitors without permission from the government in Beijing. This period of relative openness, lasting until the Chinese once again invaded in 1950, allowed for several swashbuckling expeditions to the region.

**Chapter 5: Expeditions and Adventurers**

"'Lama, tell me of Shambhala!'

'But you Westerners know nothing about Shambhala—you wish to know nothing

---

22 "China Seizes on a Dark Chapter for Tibet" by Edward Wong, in the *New York Times* , August 9th, 2010. Accessed online at: http://www.nytimes.com/2010/08/10/world/asia/10gyantse.html?_r=0

[...] you pronounce this sacred word in vain.'

'Lama, I do not ask about Shambhala aimlessly. Everywhere, people know of this
great symbol under different names. Our scientists seek each spark concerning this
remarkable realm. [...] We sense how, under secret symbols, a great truth is
concealed. Truly, the ardent scientist desires to know all about Kalachakra.'" –
Nicholas Roerich, introduction of *Shambhala, the Resplendent* (1928)

The 1903-1904 expedition was a harbinger of things to come. For the first time, a serious party
of Westerners had penetrated Tibet and the so-called "Forbidden City" of Lhasa and brought
back accounts of their journeys. This established a pent-up fascination with Tibet that was
finally given an opening in 1913 when the Chinese Revolution occurred and the Chinese state
finally lost its hold on the region, as well as its ability to keep peripheral areas like Tibet under
its control. Up until the re-assertion of Chinese dominance in 1951, Tibet attracted parties of
visitors from around the world who came seeking many things, including political influence,
military power, botanical samples, evidence for racial theories, and enlightenment. Just as often
as not, they also came seeking a hidden valley that eventually came to be known as Shangri-La.

The Russians were not newcomers to Siberia, as they had been expanding eastward for
generations. Even before the 1918 Bolshevik Revolution, they had been nibbling on the edges of
the Chinese/Tibetan sphere of influence. In 1914, soon after the Chinese Revolution, the
Russians encouraged the Tuvans to rebel from Chinese control and set up their own state as a
Russian protectorate. The Tuvans are a Buddhist Mongol people from a region just north of
modern-day Mongolia, and they eventually formed a People's Republic of Tuva between 1921
and its annexation in 1944.[23]

However, after the 1918 Bolshevik Revolution, Russian interest in Central Asia in general and
Tibet in particular grew. The Soviet leadership sought world revolution and aimed to expand
their influence across first Asia and then the world. Despite being avowed atheists, they would
not shy away from using the myth of Shambhala to their advantage whenever possible.

The first Soviet expedition to Tibet was planned as early as 1918 and was finally carried out in
1921-1922. It was headed up by V.A. Khomutnikov, an ethnic Kalymyk[24], and it traveled to
Lhasa via Mongolia. Khomutnikov brought radio to give to the Dalai Lama and fielded requests
by the government in Lhasa to give help in making firearms, but in the end, no envoy was sent to
avoid angering the British.

However, this was far from the end of Russian interest in Tibet[25]. Around the same time as

---

23 "Tuva: Russia's Tibet or the Next Lithuania?" by Ronald McMullen, accessed online at:
http://www.fotuva.org/misc/mcmullen.html
24 Like the Tuvans and Buryats, the Kalmyks are a group of Mongol-descendents who practice Tibetan Buddhism
within the political boundaries of Russia.

Khomutnikov's expedition in the region, there was another Russian who was fascinated by Tibet. Except this individual saw himself and his political philosophy as the embodiment of the Shambhala myth itself. He was the "Mad Baron", Nikolai von Ungern-Sternberg.[26]

The 1920s in northeast and central Asia was a time of great uncertainty and conflict as the great powers - Russia, Japan, China and Britain - all struggled for position and influence, not to mention attempting to undermine their opponent's resources. The Chinese were largely on the wane in the first half of the 20th century, while the Soviet Union was on the rise. Likewise, the British aimed to protect their Indian colonies and their allies in Iran, while the Japanese sought to increase their control over regions like Mongolia and Manchuria. At the same time, in the wake of World War I, the Russian Civil War and growing global Communist sympathies, there was great uncertainty, movement of people and access to arms.

The myth of Shambhala unexpectedly came to fore during this period in Mongolia. The Mongols were (and, largely, still are) Tibetan Buddhists and looked to Tibet for spiritual authority. They were also inheritors of the Shambhala story. The traditional ruler of Mongolia had the title "Jebtsundamba" (also called the "Bogd Khan"), who like the Dalai Lama was believed to be a reincarnation of a Buddha, and for centuries Mongolia, like Tibet, oscillated between being a Chinese puppet state and having some autonomy. After the chaos of the fall of the Qing Dynasty in China, Chinese power was withdrawn from the area. By the 1920s, the vagaries of war and the weakness of the Chinese opened an opportunity for the 8th Jebtsundamba to attempt to seize power. His ally in this mission was a man known as the "Mad Baron": Roman Nikolai Maximilian von Ungern-Sternberg. Of German ancestry but born in Estonia (then part of the Russian Empire), Baron Ungern had sided with the White army against the Bolsheviks during the Russian Civil War and had retreated to the steppes as the war turned against his side.

Unique for his time period and, along with his penchant for butchery, part of the reason for his moniker "mad" was that Ungern was a passionate Tibetan Buddhist. In fact, he believed himself to be Kalki, the general prophesied in the Shambhala tales to restore Buddhist rule to Central Asia. His forces aided the Jebtsundamba to power, and he ruled with a combination of anti-Bolshevism, Buddhist fundamentalism, anti-Semitism and raw cruelty. However, his reign was short-lived when he was killed a little over a month later, allegedly by his own troops.

---

25 *Soviet Russia and Tibet: The Debacle of Secret Diplomacy, 1918-1930s* (2003) by Alexandre Andreyev. Brill Press. pp 144
26 "Mongolia and the Madman" by Jason Goodwin, in *The New York Times* February 20th, 2009. Accessed online at: http://www.nytimes.com/2009/02/22/books/review/Goodwin-t.html

The Mad Baron

In 1924, the second Soviet expedition was sent out by Comintern, the governing body of international communism, this time headed by SS Borisov. This group reached Lhasa and remained in the city for three months without reaching any agreements with the Dalai Lama. The third Soviet expedition was organized by KGB Commissar Gleb Ivanovich Bokii and Aleksandr Barchenko in the 1920s and attempted to leave in 1925 but failed to reach its destination.[27] The final Soviet expedition of the 1920s traveled between 1926 and 1927, headed by A.P. Chapchayev. Chapchayev met a more hostile Dalai Lama, who asked about mistreatment of Buddhists at the hands of the Soviets.[28]

Around this time, an independent Russian expedition departed from British India. It was headed by Nicholas Roerich and traveled throughout central Asia between 1925 and 1929. Roerich was an émigré who fled the Bolshevik Revolution to New York, and he was a well-known painter and philosophical writer of the time period. His interests included Theosophy and Buddhism, and he wrote an entire book on the subject entitled *Shambhala the Resplendent*[29]. In *Shambhala*, he interpreted Tibetan myths and spirituality using his own ideas, which today are seen as forerunners to New Age beliefs. It seems that Roerich viewed himself as a self-

---

27 *Red Shambhala: Magic, Prophecy, and Geopolitics in the Heart of Asia* by Andrei Znamenski (2011)
28 *Historical Dictionary of Mongolia* by Alan J.K. Sanders (2010) pp 689
29 The text of *Shambhala* can be found on the Nicholas Roerich Museum Website: http://www.roerich.org/roerich-writings-shambhala.php

appointed Buddhist messiah and possibly as the prophesied Kalki. He believed his native Russia was Shambhala[30], and his paintings captured this spirit, with cold, surreal, mystical depictions of mountains, enlightened masters and ice fields.

**Roerich**

The Japanese also supported the Jebtsundamba and took up the mantle of Shambhala, portraying their realm as the inheritors of this ancient Buddhist tradition. However, the local Communist party eventually gained power in the area and kept the monarch for a few years as a figurehead. In 1932, there was a brutal war called the "Shambhala War" in Mongolia, which saw fighting between the Chinese Republic, which was backed by the spiritual authority of the Panchen Lama (the second-most important Lama in Tibet after the Dalai Lama), the Soviet-backed Mongols, and the Japanese Empire in their colony in neighboring Manchuria. At one time or another, all three powers invoked the myth of Shambhala to attempt to legitimize their presence in the region and to cast their enemies as the prophesied invaders. The Soviets eventually won out, and after they no longer needed propaganda or supposed mythological assistance once their military power was unassailable, they turned their back on Buddhism and the Shambhala myth. Even still, the Japanese did send one final expedition (largely for military intelligence) into the mountain kingdom in 1939[31].

---

30 "Red Star over Shambhala", by Richard Spence accessed online at
   http://www.newdawnmagazine.com/Article/Red_Star_Over_Shambhala.html

It was in the immediate wake of this short and nasty war that James Hilton published *Lost Horizon* in 1933, where he first introduced the term "Shangri-La." This novel was converted to a film of the same title in 1937 and directed by Frank Capra, who is today most famous for *It's a Wonderful Life* (1946). While information about Tibet had been available to those interested in expeditions, especially readers of *National Geographic Magazine* (in publication since 1888), the novel and film brought these ideas to a wider audience.

Another group with interest in Tibet in the final days before World War II were the Nazis, who had been in control of Germany since 1933. Years before the war, the Nazi regime was already positioning Germany to be a competitor with the other great powers of Europe in all matters. For instance, they sent an elaborate 1939 expedition to Antarctica to establish a claim on that continent[32], and they invested heavily in the Olympic Games, most famously with the massive pageantry of the 1936 Games in Berlin.[33] The Nazis also produced a stunning 1937 World's Fair pavilion at the Exposition Internationale des Arts et Techniques dans la Vie Moderne in Paris.

An expedition to Tibet was a natural addition to this campaign for power and status, since Tibet was geographically isolated and was not colonized by any of the other great powers which might strenuously oppose a German incursion.[34] Moreover, other great powers had sent expeditions to the region before and had attracted scientific and anthropological attention. There was a sense of cultural prestige attached to the expeditions.

However, there was something else to Nazi interest in Tibet aside from these pragmatic concerns. Many elite Nazi leaders had developed elaborate belief systems involving what would today be considered esoteric or mystical connections, especially involving the origins and fate of the "Aryan Race." Many of these theories held that the Aryans originated in central Asia, perhaps even in Tibet itself, and this belief system was mixed with plans for the Aryans to access mystical energy called "vril" to catapult themselves into the status of "supermen." The myth of Shambhala was compared to German ideas of a racial homeland called "Thule" or "Hyperborea", and scholars in Germany believed that there may be a shared origin. The fact that the Tibetans had long used swastikas as religious icons further attracted the Nazis.

All of this factored into the First Nazi Expedition, which journeyed from May 1938 - August 1939, ostensibly as a response to an invitation from the Tibetan Government for Germany to

31 "Exploitation of the of Shambhala Legend for Control of Mongolia" by Alexander Berzin (2003), accessed online at:
   http://www.berzinarchives.com/web/en/archives/advanced/kalachakra/shambhala/exploitation_shambala_legend_mongolia.html
32 "Neuschwabenland, the Last German Colony" (2007) by Frank Jacobs, accessed online at:
   http://bigthink.com/strange-maps/88-neuschwabenland-the-last-german-colony
33 "1936 Olympics and the Struggle for Influence" by Nathan Huegen, video accessed online at: http://www.c-spanvideo.org/program/Olympicsan
34 At this point - the height of European Imperialism - there were precious few places in the Old World that were not colonized: Liberia, Siam, Japan, China itself and Iran for instance.

participate in New Year's celebrations in Lhasa. The head of the expedition was Ernst Schäfer, an SS officer who had already been to Tibet twice, once in 1931-2 and again in 1934-6. While the expedition had a botanical component, another side was dedicated to racial research, hoping to provide evidence for theories of the Aryan origin and, presumably, for links to Shambhala and the Aryan homeland[35].

**Schafer in Tibet in 1938**

On the eve of the war, the Nazis sent out a second group called the "Nanga Parbat Expedition,"

---

35 "The Nazi Connection with Shambhala and Tibet" by Alexander Berzin (2003), accessed online at: http://www.berzinarchives.com/web/en/archives/advanced/kalachakra/shambhala/nazi_connection_shambhala_ti bet.html

which sought to climb Nanga Parbat, the 9th tallest mountain in the world. Leaving in May of 1939, they were captured by the British in India in September of that year before reaching the summit. Two members of the four-man team, Heinrich Harrer and Peter Aufschnaiter , escaped British internment in 1944 and fled to Tibet. They remained in Tibet throughout the war, and Harrer became an adviser to the Dalai Lama himself, eventually living in the country for seven years. When he returned to Austria in 1952 after the Chinese invasion, he wrote the famous book *Seven Years in Tibet.* This second expedition was less about racial theories and Aryan links to Shambhala and more about proving the physical superiority of German athletes. This type of trip was in the vein of British mountaineering expeditions to Everest in 1921, 1922, 1924 and on into the 1930s, and also in the spirit of the 1936 Summer Olympics, which were a celebration of the strength, virility and superiority of German men.

**Harrer**

There were a number of other expeditions traversing the Himalayas during this era. The British public was fascinated by the travels of Scotsman George Forrest, who remained in the region between 1906 and his death in 1932. He was followed by the American Joseph Francis Charles Rock, who journeyed through the area in 1924. Both men were botanists whose primary interest was bringing seeds and samples back to a public fascinated not only with the tales of their journeys (which were avidly devoured) but also with those very plant samples. Forrest alone delivered 30,000 specimens to the Royal Botanical Garden in Edinburgh[36]. Both men

---

36 "George Forrest" at the homepage of the Royal Botanical Garden Edinburgh

published accounts of their work, and Rock in particular spent time on the lecture circuit, bringing his striking photographs with him for public consumption. These men tended to start in southeast China, especially in rhododendron-rich Yunnan province, and then moved north and west into Tibet.[37]

## Chapter 6: Tibet comes West

"Here's your reward for working so hard

Gone is the lavatory in the back yard

Gone are the days when you dreamed of that car

You just want to sit in your Shangri-La" – The Kinks, "Shangri-La"

One more expedition ended this period of Tibetan history: the invasion of the Chinese People's Liberation army in 1950-1951, an event that led to the eventual annexation of Tibet in 1959 and the flight of the Dalai Lama and most of his court into exile in the same year. These events had the simultaneous effect of ending the expeditions by completely sealing Tibet from outside influence but also of opening the possibility of the outside world for more direct encounters with Tibetan Buddhism. As opposed to a second-hand encounter through Theosophy or expedition reports, the West could now more easily meet the Dalai Lama and the exiled leadership.

http://www.rbge.org.uk/science/herbarium/about-the-collections/collectors#g_forrest
37 *The Paper Road: Archive and Experience in the Botanical Exploration of West China and Tibet* by Erik Mueggler (2011)

## The 14th Dalai Lama

When the Dalai Lama fled China, he chose to lead his followers into nearby India.  While this may have been his only option at the time, given the Soviet Union's hostility to Buddhism and its alliance with China, it follows the old patterns of Tibet existing in the interstices between these great empires.  The Indians themselves were struggling with China for position and authority in Central Asia, which reached its height three years later in the 1962 Sino-Indian War over disputed areas within the Tibetan Plateau, especially the Aksai Chin region.  Since that time, the Tibetan administration in exile has built monasteries and communities concentrated on the southern slopes of the Himalayas and used this position as a base for expanding their spiritual and political influence around the world, much to the ongoing frustration of the Chinese government.

The era of expeditions was directly tied to a low point in Chinese influence.  The British invasion of 1903-1904 was possible because the Qing had largely withdrawn from the region, and when the Chinese maintained a presence in the region from 1910-1913, further expeditions were impossible.  The on again-off again nature of Chinese influence is very much a feature of Tibetan history, with the relations with their powerful eastern neighbor having a great influence upon their autonomy.  However, despite the "closing" of Tibet in 1959 and the presence of "legitimate" defenders of the myth, the fascination of the West with Tibet and Shangri-La morphed when direct contact facilitated an easier transmission of knowledge to Western audiences.

The largest impact of this era was the widespread use of the term Shangri-La itself.  By the 1950s, the mythical valley's name became a household word in the English-speaking world, and according to contemporary dictionary definitions, it means a hidden place characterized by peace, contentment or a haven of goodness[38].  As that definition suggests, the usage of the term Shangri-La has even been separated from direct connection to Tibet, instead coming to be used for any location with an air of the exotic that was characterized by a relaxing retreat from the world. Some of the first uses were amongst the wealthy to denote places of escape.  For instance, the heiress Doris Duke had an Islamic-style mansion built for herself in 1937 which she named "Shangri-La". The wide gulf between North African-inspired buildings and a Tibetan name did not appear to bother Duke, nor has it bothered the Islamic art foundation that still runs the facility.[39]  Similarly, an expensive art deco hotel built in California's ritzy town of Santa Monica was completed in 1939 and also bore the valley's name without having any other nod to Tibet.[40]  In 1942, a botanic garden was founded with the name in Texas[41], as was a coastal resort in

---

38 "Shangri-La" at Dictionary.com, accessed online at: http://dictionary.reference.com/browse/Shangri-La
39 Shangri La Center for Islamic Arts and Cultures Homepage.  Accessed online at: http://www.shangrilahawaii.org/
40 Hotel Shangrila Homepage.  Accessed online at: http://www.shangrila-hotel.com/
41 Shangri La Botanical Gardens and Nature Center Homepage.  Accessed online at: http://starkculturalvenues.org/shangrilagardens/

Uruguay, well outside the English-speaking world, in 1946.

**A room in Doris Duke's "Shangri-La"**

American President Franklin Roosevelt seemed to have been so enamored with the term that he originally used it for the presidential retreat that is now called Camp David. He also famously used it to describe the origin point for the Doolittle Raiders who were the first pilots to bomb Tokyo during the Second World War. Ironically, for a name associated with tranquility, it was also the name of an American aircraft carrier during the war as well.

From this high point in the 1940s and 1950s, the term began to decline in use and also lost most of its significance in the everyday sense. There was a 1960 film starring Claude Rains as the "High Lama" and Richard Basehart as a European explorer[42] that was based off of Hilton's book and brought the term into cinemas around the country, but after that the connection to Tibet began to wane. In fact, Shangri-La's association with exoticism had become optional by 1969, as "Shangri-La" came to stand for the "home as castle" concept and a celebration of comfortable living in suburban America. The all-girl group "The Shangri-Las" sang bubble-gum pop songs

---

42 "Shangri-La (1960)" at the Internet Movie Database, accessed online at:
   http://www.imdb.com/title/tt0335407/?ref_=fn_al_tt_3

like "Leader of the Pack" and "Remember" in the 1960s, which had no apparent connection to the mythological valley. Besides, the original concept of Shangri-La was in contrast to their "bad girl" image. A 1973 remake of *Lost Horizon* for the big screen was a blip in this overall decline[43]. While the term never faded completely from use in American English, these musical tributes to the name serve as a bookend for the termination of one era of interest in Shangri-La and opened the door for the next, contemporary period of interest.

## Chapter 7: Tibet and Shangri-La Today

> "By way of explaining what we've been doing and are about to do, I'm going to first talk to you a little bit about the country called Tibet. Tibet is bordered on the southeast by Burma, on the south by India and Nepal, on the west by India and Kashmir and on the north and east by China. It is almost completely surrounded by mountain ranges. An extremely spiritual country, practicing a form of Buddhism known as Tibetan Buddhism, for many centuries the leader of Tibet has been known as the Dalai Lama [...] Following a Tibetan uprising against the Chinese in 1959, the Dalai Lama was forced to flee for his life to India and has lived in exile ever since.
>
> Following a dream I had three years ago, I have become deeply moved by the plight of the Tibetan people and have been filled with a desire to help them. I also awoke from this same dream realizing that I had subconsciously gained knowledge of a certain deductive technique, involving mind-body coordination operating hand-in-hand with the deepest levels of intuition." -Agent Dale Cooper from the television show *Twin Peaks* (1990-1991), Episode 2[44]

While aiming to be humorous, this memorable quote from the seminal television show *Twin Peaks* expresses a popular conception of the Tibetan people, religion and political movement that emerged only after the flight of the Dalai Lama to India. In the decades since then, the Dalai Lama and his government-in-exile, the Central Tibetan Administration, have constructed a world-wide network of Buddhist organizations, monasteries, publishing houses, retreat centers, charitable foundations and political pressure groups. This interest reached a zenith in the late 1980s and early 1990s, culminating with the Dalai Lama being awarded the Nobel Peace Prize in 1989[45] and the creation of the Tibetan Freedom Concerts in 1996.

The existence of this network has facilitated the most important transformation in the recent history of the story of Shangri-La, because the Western public no longer had to rely upon the

---

43 "Lost Horizon (1973)" at the Internet Movie Database, accessed online at:
   http://www.imdb.com/media/rm1541381888/tt0070337
44 Script accessed online at: http://www.lynchnet.com/tp/tp02.html
45 "The 14th Dalai Lama" at the homepage of the Nobel Prize. Accessed online at:
   http://www.nobelprize.org/nobel_prizes/peace/laureates/1989/lama-bio.html

interpretations and theories of visitors to Tibet who returned and gave their own interpretations of myths like Shambhala. Instead, they could now read the Dalai Lama's words in an official translation, listen to his speeches, visit numerous Buddhist establishments, and even check websites of fellow devotees and religious institutions. The Shambhala Myth continues to be important even in the present; for example, it has been adopted by the Shambhala Buddhist Community, a network of 170 meditation centers and study groups located primarily in North America and Western Europe. The community was founded by Chögyam Trungpa Rinpoche, a monk who fled Tibet along with the Dalai Lama[46]. The legendary valley also gave its name to *Shambhala Sun*, a Tibetan Buddhist magazine[47].

These two institutions are examples of the return of "Shambhala" over "Shangri-La" and a growing prominence of Buddhist influence on the myth. But it is not only the Tibetan Buddhists in exile who utilize the myth, nor has their presence completely erased previous interpretations. Shangri-La/Shambhala has become a popular subject for New Age philosophy and theology as well. These writings focus upon the "mysteries" and draw upon all elements of the story. There is talk of Nazi secret societies sending covert missions to hunt the Ascended Masters, of the mystical powers of the monks, and of the spiritual power that emanates from it.[48] A popular example is the book *The Secret of Shambhala: In Search of the Eleventh Insight*, written by James Redfield and published in 1999. The book is part of the world-famous *The Celestine Prophecy* trilogy, which fuses Eastern religion (especially Buddhism) with Western New Age ideas and became a New York Times bestseller. Western visitors to Nepal and Bhutan, who often come with an interest in Buddhism, esoteric arts and New Age spirituality, are offered services like the "Shambhala Tours" travel agency and the "Shambhala Healing Arts" massage and herbalist clinic. There are even modern-day expeditions that set out to discover Shangri-La, such as the one that was the basis of the 2007 documentary "Finding Shangri-La[49]."

As the West's interest continues to make clear, Tibet continues to be a cultural touchstone that connects the globe. Tibet today is considered by many to be more spiritual, enlightened and oppressed than the rest of the world, and its connection to "intuitive" practices like New Age religion and other mystical movements is unlikely to fade anytime soon. With that, it's safe to assume that the myths of Shangri-La and Shambhala will continue to be prominent.

**Bibliography**

Allen, Charles. (1999). The Search for Shangri-La: A Journey into Tibetan History. (2000)

---

46 "Shambhala: Making Enlightened Society Possible," organization homepage accessed online at http://www.shambhala.org/index.php
47 *Shambhala Sun* Homepage accessed online at: http://www.shambhalasun.com/
48 For example, see: http://rumorfriends.blogspot.com/2012/03/mysteries-of-kingdom-of-shambhala.html
49 "Finding Shangri-La (2007)" at the Internet Movie Database, accessed online at: http://www.imdb.com/title/tt1365603/?ref_=fn_al_tt_8

Beckwith, Christopher I. The Tibetan Empire in Central Asia: A History of the Struggle for Great Power among Tibetans, Turks, Arabs, and Chinese during the Early Middle Ages' (1987)

Goldstein, Melvyn C. A History of Modern Tibet, 1913–1951: The Demise of the Lamaist State (1989)

Kapstein, Matthew T. The Tibetans (2006)

Stein, R. Tibetan Civilization (1972)

Teltscher, Kate. The High Road to China: George Bogle, the Panchen Lama and the First British Expedition to Tibet (2006)